WEST CHICAGO PUBLIC LIBRARY DISTRICT
3 6653 00177 6057

11/08

P9-CML-084

$24.00

Amazing Animals
Elephants

Please visit our web site at www.garethstevens.com.
For a free catalog describing our list of high-quality books, call 1-800-542-2595 (USA) or 1-800-387-3178 (Canada).
Our fax: 1-877-542-2596

Library of Congress Cataloging-in-Publication Data

Albee, Sarah.
Elephants / by Sarah Albee.
p. cm.— (Amazing Animals)
Originally published: Pleasantville, NY: Reader's Digest Young Families, c2006.
Includes bibliographical references and index.
ISBN-10: 0-8368-9096-5 ISBN-13: 978-0-8368-9096-9 (lib. bdg.)
1. Elephants—Juvenile literature. I. Title.
QL737.P98A42 2009
599.67—dc22 2008013381

This edition first published in 2009 by
Gareth Stevens Publishing
A Weekly Reader® Company
1 Reader's Digest Road
Pleasantville, NY 10570-7000 USA

Gareth Stevens Senior Managing Editor: Lisa M. Herrington
Gareth Stevens Creative Director: Lisa Donovan
Gareth Stevens Art Director: Ken Crossland
Gareth Stevens Associate Editor: Amanda Hudson

Consultant: Robert E. Budliger (Retired), NY State Department of Environmental Conservation

Photo Credits
Front cover: IT Stock. Title page: Dynamic Graphics, Inc. Contents: Dynamic Graphics, Inc. pages 6-7: IT Stock. pages 8-9: Brand X Pictures. pages 10-11: IT Stock. page 12: Brand X Pictures. page 13: Digital Vision. pages 14-15: Corbis Corporation. page 16: Brand X Pictures. page 17: Dynamic Graphics, Inc. page 18 (upper left and large picture): IT Stock. page 19: Dynamic Graphics, Inc. page 20: IT Stock. page 21: Digital Vision. pages 22-23: Digital Vision. page 24: Brand X Pictures. page 25: Nova Development Corporation. pages 26-27: PhotoDisc. page 28: Brand X Pictures. page 29: Nova Development Corporation. pages 30-31: Dynamic Graphics, Inc. pages 32-33: Digital Vision. pages 34-35: PhotoDisc. page 36: IT Stock. pages 37-39: Digital Vision. page 40: istockphoto.com/Steffen Foerster. page 41: JupiterImages. page 42: Digital Vision. pages 44-45: Dynamic Graphics, Inc. page 46: Nova Development Corporation. Back cover: Brand X Pictures.

Printed in the United States of America

1 2 3 4 5 6 7 8 9 10 09 08

Amazing Animals

Elephants

By Sarah Albee

Contents

Chapter 1

An Elephant Story

Little Elephant looked up. Dark clouds were zooming across the sky. The long, dry season was coming to an end at last. Her mother stood nearby, along with several of Little Elephant's aunts, all of them keeping a close eye on their little ones.

Soon Little Elephant's mother would be ready to have another baby. Little Elephant couldn't wait to have a new brother or sister to play with!

The elephants in the herd stomped and snorted. Drops of rain began to fall. The rain felt wonderful!

For the next week or so, the herd trudged across the wide-open plains. Now that the rainy season had arrived, the elephants were following Big Elephant to the river. She was the largest elephant in the herd and had lived a long time. She knew just where to go. And she was Little Elephant's great-aunt!

Is it true that elephants never forget?

Elephants have large brains and good memories. Older elephants remember paths that lead to good feeding areas and water holes. They often recognize distant relatives.

Little Elephant's group arrived at the marshlands near the river. There was plenty of food and water for everyone. Soon Little Elephant spotted another group of elephants.

Big Elephant had been sending signals to the other group as they crossed the grassy plain. The other elephants had signaled back, telling Big Elephant where they were.

Little Elephant greeted the young elephants in the group. They roared and rumbled. Then Little Elephant and her friends jumped into the muddy water. They splashed and picked up gobs of mud with their **trunks**, slapping it against their bodies to cool off.

Fun Fact

Elephants are the second tallest animals in the world! The tallest are giraffes.

Suddenly Big Elephant let out a bellow. All the elephants stomped and trumpeted with joy. A new baby had been born to Little Elephant's mother!

When Big Elephant gave the signal, Little Elephant hurried over to greet her new baby brother. Their mother was gently helping him to stand up on his wobbly legs. He was learning to balance himself on his four legs. Little Elephant touched him gently with her trunk. She had so much to teach her little brother about being an elephant!

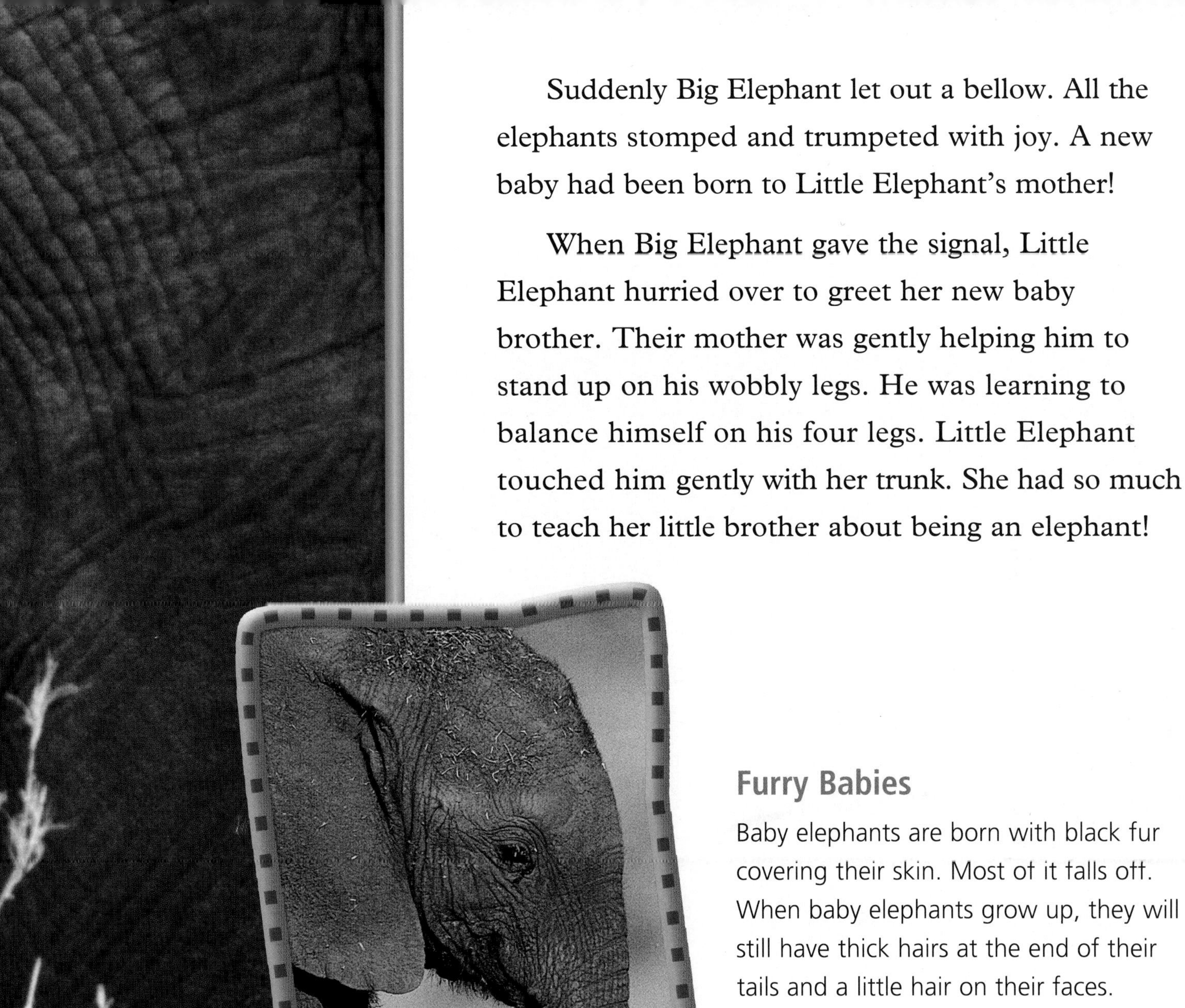

Furry Babies

Baby elephants are born with black fur covering their skin. Most of it falls off. When baby elephants grow up, they will still have thick hairs at the end of their tails and a little hair on their faces.

Like lions, bears, and humans, elephants belong to the group of animals scientists call **mammals**. All mammals have hair.

Chapter 2

The Body of an Elephant

The ears of African elephants are the same shape as the continent of Africa!

The Biggest

Elephants are the largest land animals in the world.

Two Kinds of Elephants

There are two kinds of elephants. One lives in Asia. The other lives in Africa. The biggest difference between the two is the size of their ears. Asian elephants have smaller, pointier ears. African elephants have huge ears that are rounder in shape and rise above their necks.

Asian elephants are smaller than African elephants. Asian elephants are about 9 feet (2.7 meters) tall at the shoulder. African elephants are 10 to 13 feet (3 to 4 m) tall.

Asian elephants are different in shape, too. They have a rounder body with a humped back. The backs of African elephants have a slight dip in the middle.

All African elephants have **tusks**. The tusks are very big. In Asia, only male elephants have tusks.

Asian Elephants

Asian elephants are smaller than African elephants and have smaller ears. They have two bumps on their foreheads.

Fingertips!

An African elephant's trunk has two flaps at the tip that work together like your thumb and pointer finger to pick up small objects. In Asia, an elephant's trunk has just one flap. It also works like a finger.

The trunk of an elephant serves as the animal's hand and nose. It can do many amazing things.

A Hunk of a Trunk

The trunk of an elephant can lift a heavy log or pluck a single blade of grass. It can bend, stretch, and curl. It can suck up, spray, or hold water. It is loaded with taste and smell sensors—elephants can smell water miles away. The trunk caresses other elephants, maybe to show affection. The main task of a trunk, though, is to carry food and water to the elephant's mouth.

The trunk is part of the elephant's nose and upper lip. It can be as long as 6 feet (1.8 m) and has no bones in it. It is made completely of muscle. Some scientists think it has more than 40,000 separate muscles.

What's Up?

Elephants use their trunks to touch each other or say hello. They may also twist their trunks together, like people shaking hands!

Giant-Size Teeth

Tusks are giant-size **incisor** teeth. They continue to grow throughout the animal's lifetime. Tusks are used for digging, peeling bark from trees, lifting, and when necessary, as weapons. In Africa, all elephants grow tusks. Among Asian elephants, only males develop tusks.

Elephants also have four huge teeth inside their mouths. One tooth can weigh more than 11 pounds (5 kilograms)! Like your molars, elephant teeth have ridges for grinding up food. When a tooth gets worn out, a new one grows in. Elephants grow six sets of teeth in their lifetime. The last set grows in when the animal is about 40 years old.

Ivory Tusks

Unfortunately for elephants, humans have prized **ivory** over the centuries. Because elephants are an endangered **species**, the business of selling ivory has been **banned**. Still, illegal ivory hunters exist.

Elephants use one tusk more than the other, just as we use one hand more than the other. The main tusk is rounder at the tip and sometimes shorter than the other tusk.

On Tiptoe

Elephants are very sure-footed. They step quickly and almost soundlessly, which is surprising in such large animals!

Elephants have toes, but we can only see some of the toenails. They walk by putting their toes down first, then the heel. The elephant's weight is supported by the tip of the toe and a squishy foot pad in the heel that acts as a cushion.

The foot pad is a spongy layer of skin that expands as the foot is placed down. The ridges on the bottoms of an elephant's feet grip the ground like a person's hiking boots do.

Elephants can support their weight on their hind legs. This means they can reach leaves on tall trees.

Elephants can walk forward and backward. They can run and swim, but they cannot jump.

On the Go

Elephants walk several miles in a day. They usually move at about 4 to 5 miles (6 to 8 km) an hour, but they can sprint for a short distance at a rate of 30 miles (48 km) per hour. That's faster than the fastest human marathon runners, who run only 13 miles (21 km) per hour!

The skin of elephants is very thick. It is also very sensitive. An elephant can feel a fly landing on its skin!

Wrinkly Skin

Elephant skin is very wrinkly. The wrinkles come in handy. They allow the animal to move about freely, as if dressed in a roomy suit of clothes, to bend and kneel and run. The cracks and grooves in the skin trap water and mud. This helps keep the elephant cool on hot days. The mud helps prevent sunburn, too.

Another word for an elephant is a **pachyderm** (pronounced PACK ih derm). It is the Greek word for "thick-skinned."

"Ear" Conditioning

Elephant ears are natural air conditioners. The ears have lots of blood vessels close to the surface of the skin. As air moves over the ears, it cools the blood vessels. Cooler blood then circulates around the elephant's body. African elephant ears can wave like huge fans, letting body heat escape.

Chapter 3

Meals and Baths

Time to Eat!

Elephants can spend up to 16 hours a day eating!

What Elephants Eat

Elephants need a lot of food to support their huge size. Elephants are **herbivores**, which means they eat only plants. In addition to grasses, leaves, and fruits, elephants eat twigs and tree bark.

Like other herbivores, elephants crave salt and other minerals that plants do not provide. So elephants eat soil, which has the nutrients they need. They dig with their tusks and grind the soil and rock into powder with their teeth.

Elephants in search of food can be destructive when food is scarce. They will strip shrubs of leaves and knock down trees to get the leaves on top. But elephants change the landscape in good ways, too. By eating shrubs and small trees, they thin out wooded areas, letting in sunshine for new plants to grow.

Three Meals a Day

Although elephants spend most of their time eating, they eat three "meals" a day just like you. They eat in the morning, afternoon, and night.

At noon, when the sun is hottest, elephants find shade and sometimes doze while standing up. At night, they lie down on their side to sleep.

Water Wonders

Elephants need a lot of water to survive, and they never go very far from it. To drink, an elephant draws up water with its trunk and squirts the water into its mouth. A baby elephant has to kneel down to drink until it learns how to use its trunk.

Elephants love to soak in watering holes. Soaking in deep water lets the elephant take weight off its feet and legs.

Elephants also love to swim. They can swim several miles at one time. They may even use their trunks as snorkels.

During periods of **drought**, it can be hard to find water. Older elephants will loosen the soil with their tusks and use their trunks to dig for water below the surface. Other animals know that elephants can find hidden water, so they often follow elephants, hoping to benefit from their well-digging services.

Elephants love to play in the water. They splash and spray to cool down and to get rid of pesky insects.

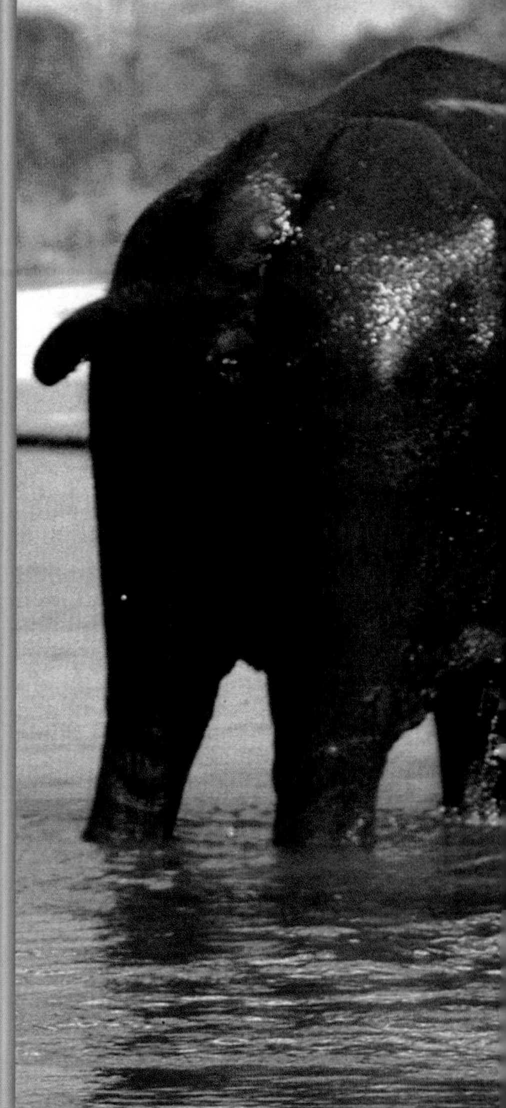

Mud Baths

After bathing, elephants dust themselves with dirt or roll in the mud to coat themselves. The mud keeps the animals cool and their skin soft. It also helps protect against insects and sunburn.

Chapter 4
Elephant Families

Caring Creatures

Elephants are very caring animals. If a baby elephant takes a nap, the group will wait until it wakes up before moving on. If a member of the herd is sick or hurt, the other elephants will not leave it.

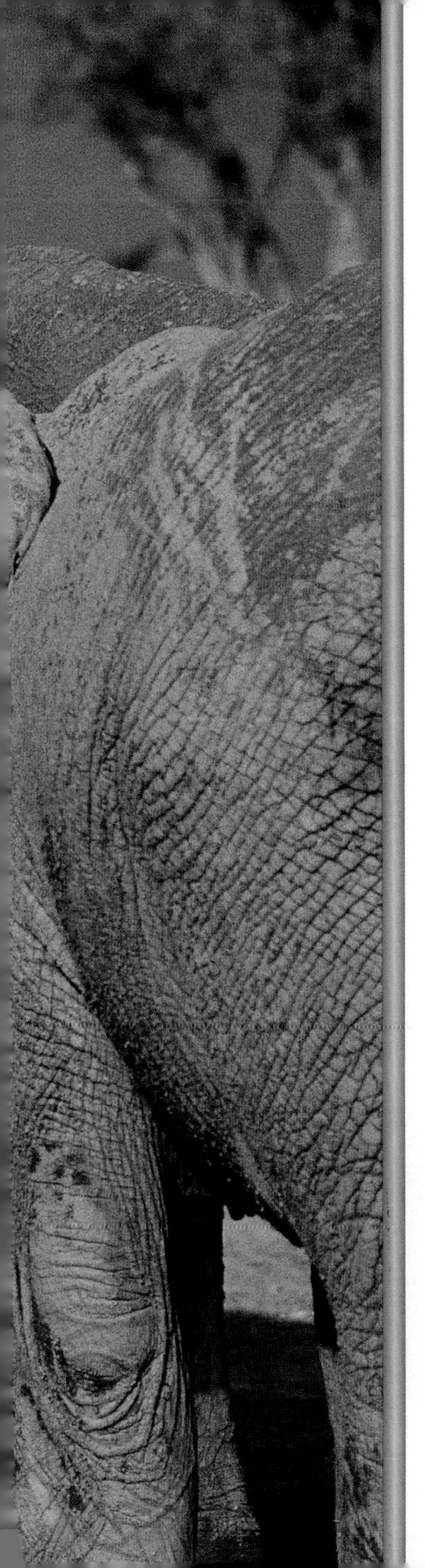

Keeping in Touch

Elephants live in small family groups of about 8 to 10 animals. The group is led by a female elephant called the **matriarch** (pronounced MAY tree ark). She is usually the oldest animal in the group. Elephants travel in groups called herds.

Elephants keep in contact with each other by sounds. Their usual call is a low rumbling noise. Humans cannot hear it, but other elephants can.

Family Ties

Female elephants stay with the group for life, but males leave at around 12 to 14 years of age to start their own families.

Elephants also communicate using body language. When they are relaxed, their trunks hang down and their ears are back. When they are angry, they flare out their ears, pull back their trunks, and point their tusks forward. Elephants warn enemies by whirling their trunks around or tossing up a cloud of dust.

Big Babies

When a mother elephant is ready to have a baby, the other elephants in the group gather around to protect her. One female helps her with the birth. Within an hour, the **calf** can stand up on its own. The elephants welcome the baby by stomping their feet and trumpeting.

The mother elephant is very protective of her baby. For the first few months, the baby elephant lives only on its mother's milk. A calf will drink about 7 gallons (26 liters) of milk a day until age two. Young elephants spend lots of time playing. Calves run, charge after birds, and play-fight.

Elephants have a long childhood. They learn from the older elephants in their group. Sisters, aunts, and grandmothers help the mothers take care of the young elephants.

A Comfort Trunk

An elephant calf sucks on its trunk for comfort just as a human baby does with his thumb!

One at a Time

Female elephants give birth to one baby elephant at a time. Scientists call the baby a calf. Female elephants may have four to six calves during their lifetime.

A baby elephant is small enough to walk under its mother's belly. A young calf often wraps its trunk around the mother's tail so the pair won't get separated from each other.

Chapter 5

Past and Future

Hyraxes don't look anything like elephants. But scientists say hyraxes (and manatees) are the closest living relatives of elephants!

Big and Small Relatives

The ancient relatives of elephants belong to a group of animals called *Proboscidea* ("animals with a trunk"). Mammoths and mastodons, which became extinct about 10,000 years ago, were part of this group.

Fast Facts About Elephants

	African Elephant	Asian Elephant
Scientific Name:	*Loxodonta africana*	*Elephas maximus*
Class:	Mammals	Mammals
Order:	Proboscidea (animals with trunks)	Proboscidea (animals with trunks)
Size:	(male) 10-13 feet (3 to 4 m) tall	(male) 9 feet (2.7 m) tall
Weight:	(male) 6 tons	(male) 5 tons
Life Span:	Up to 80 years	Up to 80 years
Habitat:	savanna, forest	forest, grassland

The closest living relatives of elephants include manatees and small, furry mammals called hyraxes. Hyraxes don't look like elephants, but they have a few things in common with them, like cushioned foot pads and large front teeth. Hyraxes live in Africa and some parts of the Middle East.

You Can Help!

You help save elephants from extinction every time you reuse or recycle paper, metal, and glass. Your effort helps to slow the rate at which elephant **habitats** are disappearing.

Elephants live in a wide range of habitats, from savannas to forests. When the sun is hottest, they look for shade.

Where Elephants Live

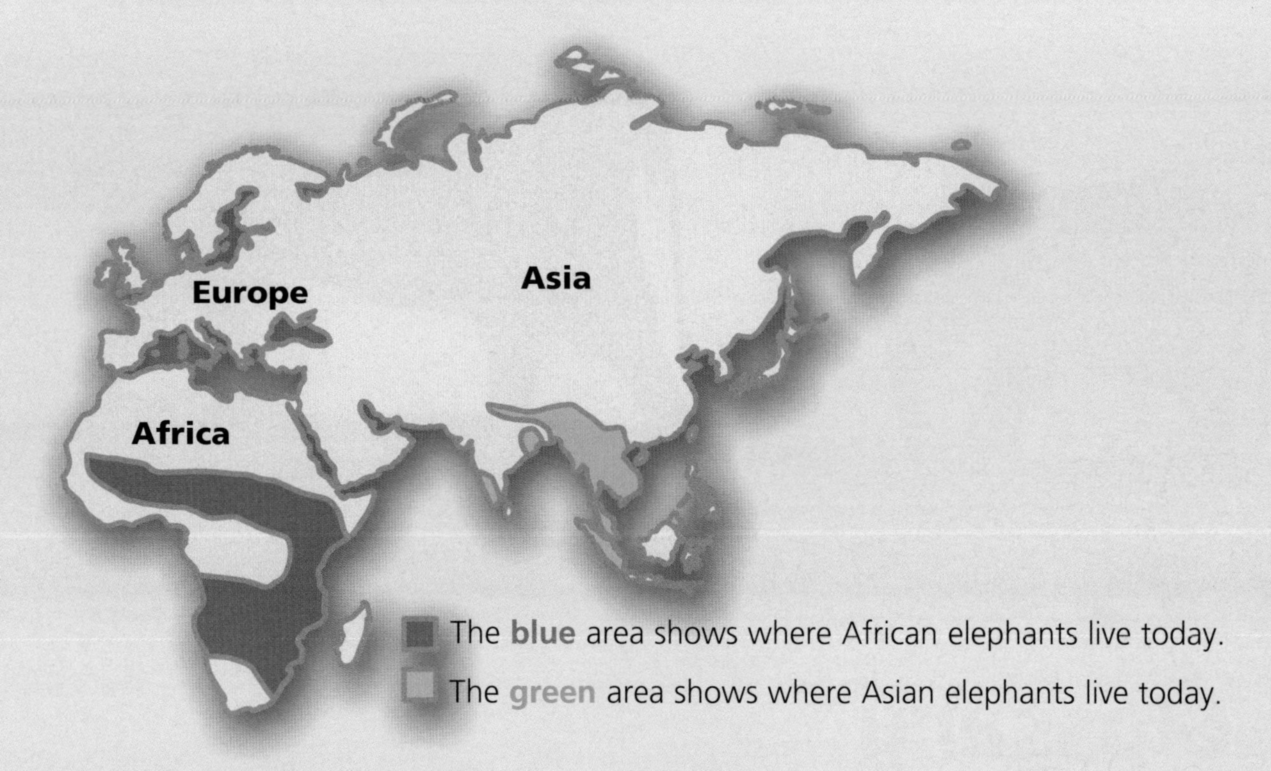

Because of their huge size, elephants do not have many **predators**. The biggest threat to elephants is humans. Elephant tusks are made of ivory, which has been prized for centuries. To take an elephant's tusks, the elephant must be killed first. The trading of ivory was banned in 1989, but ivory is still sold illegally.

Another cause of the decline in the number of elephants is the destruction of their habitats. Elephants once lived throughout Africa, but now live in just one-third of the continent. Land in Asia and Africa is being cleared for farming, lumber, mining, and buildings.

Glossary

banned — forbidden by law

calf — a young elephant

drought — a period of time during which there is little or no rain

habitat — the natural environment where an animal or plant lives

herbivore — an animal that eats only plants

incisor — a kind of tooth. An elephant's tusks are very, very long incisors

ivory — a smooth, hard white substance that forms the tusks of elephants and other animals

mammal — an animal with a backbone and hair on its body that drinks milk from its mother when it is born

Are elephants smart?

Elephants communicate with one another and take care of each other. They even use tools. For example, they pick up sticks with their trunks to scratch itches they can't reach. They dig holes for water, drink, cover the holes up with soil and branches, and return at a later time to drink again. They can learn tricks and remember them for a long time—some say forever.

matriarch — female leader of a group

pachyderm — another word for elephant. It comes from the Greek word for "thick-skinned."

predator — an animal that hunts and eats other animals to survive

proboscidea — ancient relatives of elephants that included mastodons and mammoths

savanna — a flat grassland area with scattered trees in a hot region of the world

species — a group of plants or animals that are the same in many ways

trunk — the long, flexible snout of an elephant

tusk — a very long, pointed tooth that sticks far out from the side of an animal's mouth, usually one of a pair

visible — able to be seen

Elephants: Show What You Know

How much have you learned about elephants? Grab a piece of paper and a pencil and write your answers down.

1. Elephants are the second tallest animals in the world. Which animal is the tallest?

2. What is an elephant's trunk made of?

3. What is the biggest difference between Asian elephants and Indian elephants?

4. What is the main task of an elephant's trunk?

5. How many sets of teeth do elephants grow in their lifetime?

6. What is the female leader of an elephant herd called?

7. Why does a baby elephant wrap its trunk around its mother's tail?

8. What are two of the closest living relatives of elephants?

9. What predator is the biggest threat to elephants?

10. How can you help protect elephant habitats?

1. The giraffe 2. Muscle 3. The size of their ears 4. To bring food and water to its mouth 5. 6 6. The matriarch 7. So they won't get separated 8. Hyraxes and manatees 9. Humans 10. By recycling paper, metal, and glass

For More Information

Books

Elephant. Bloom, Steve (Chronicle Books, 2006)

Elephants. Nature Watch (series). Taylor, Barbara (Lorenz Books, 2008)

Elephants. Zoobooks (series). Wexo, John Bonnett (Wildlife Education, Ltd., 2002)

Web Sites

Elephanteria

http://www.himandus.net/elephanteria

This kid-friendly site is a "Smorgasbord of Elephantine Delights." Exciting features celebrate elephants, including a "fun stuff" section with activities.

The Elephants of Africa

http://www.pbs.org/wnet/nature/elephants

Watch elephants in their natural habitat. Learn about the elephant life cycle, threats to elephants in the modern world, and much more.

Elephant Information Repository

http://elephant.elehost.com

Find the latest news about elephants all around the world. This site promises "a trunk full" of elephant information.

Publisher's note to educators and parents: Our editors have carefully reviewed these Web sites to ensure that they are suitable for children. Many Web sites change frequently, however, and we cannot guarantee that a site's future contents will continue to meet our high standards of quality and educational value. Be advised that children should be closely supervised whenever they access the Internet.

Index